Celebrities Cheer:

"Wouldn't it be wonderful if programs were always this funny!"
—Bennett Cerf

"I laughed from beginning to end."
—Arlene Francis

"At the time most of these boners happened they weren't very funny... but in this book they are hilarious!"
—Faye Emerson

"This delightful assortment of chuckles proves that people are funniest when they're being human."
—Dorothy Kilgallen

"A catalogue of unintended indiscretions before camera and microphone to lift the spirit and put a smile upon the greyest hour."
—John Daly

Laundry commercial: "We do not tear your clothes by machinery, we do it carefully by hand."

Pardon My Blooper

Former title: YOUR SLIP IS SHOWING
Newly Revised

by Kermit Schafer

Illustrated by
BERNARD THOMPSON

A FAWCETT GOLD MEDAL BOOK
Fawcett Publications, Inc., Greenwich, Conn.
Member of American Book Publishers Council, Inc.

PARDON MY BLOOPER

collected by

Kermit Schafer

for

Bloopers Inc.

creator of

Pardon My Blooper Record Albums

for

Jubilee Record Co.

Pardon My Blooper title and material copyright by Bloopers Inc., Central Valley, New York

Copyright MCMLIII Grayson Publishing Corp.
Copyright © 1959, Kermit Schafer

Some of the material in PARDON MY BLOOPER was published by Grayson Publishing Corp. under the title YOUR SLIP IS SHOWING, and has been incorporated in this edition through arrangement with that company.

All rights reserved, including the right to reproduce this book or portions thereof.

Published by Fawcett World Library,
67 West 44th Street, New York, New York 10036
Printed in the United States of America

DEDICATED

To the members of the radio and television industry who have spent anguished and painful moments, days, perhaps years reliving some of these torturous incidents. If nothing else, it is hoped that this book offers consolation and proof of the fact that they are not alone.

Kermit Schafer
Radio and TV Producer

"To err is human, to forgive divine."

Alexander Pope

Other Fawcett Gold Medal Books
by Kermit Schafer:

SUPER BLOOPERS
PRIZE BLOOPERS

STRIKE IT RICH

On "STRIKE IT RICH," popular television program produced by Walt Framer, Warren Hull, Master of Ceremonies, interviewed a five year old child whose father was in the United States Army serving in Korea. She wanted to Strike it Rich for an apartment where she would have her own bedroom; whereupon the surprised Hull asked: "With Daddy away in Korea, isn't the apartment you live in with Mommy big enough?" The child's reply was, "During the week I sleep in the bedroom with Mommy, but on the week-ends, when Uncle Charlie comes, they make me sleep on a cot in the kitchen. Anyway, he's not really my uncle."

RADIO STORY TELLER

NARRATOR: ". . . and as his trusty little donkey carried Quixote up the road, he could see the gates of the city ahead. Don Quixote's excitement rose as he contemplated the knightly adventures that awaited him." (*Time running out*) ". . . and there we leave Don Quixote, sitting on his ass, until tomorrow at the same time."

(4-H Club on the air)
"Today I would like to explain to all you boys and girls how to go about forming your own 4-H club. The chief requisite is to have an adult leader, like myself, which can be a man or woman or a combination of both."

DRAMATIC PROGRAM

GANGSTER: "Okay you rat, I've got you covered and now I'm going to drill ya."
(*Complete silence*)
GANGSTER: (*Realizing that the sound effects man has run into trouble*)
"On second thought I'm going to slit your throat."
Two shots—The sound man had located his trouble.

NEW ANNOUNCER

When Pat Adelman, program director of Station KNOW, Texas, finished preparing the day's schedule, he left it in the control room. Later he made a change—instead of Les Brown's orchestra, he substituted a religious program which was to originate from N. Y. He scratched out Les Brown's and wrote over it, Yom Kippur. When the new announcer came on shift, he picked up the schedule and exhorted his listeners to "Stay tuned for the dance music of Yom Kippur's Orchestra."[2]

COMMERCIAL CONTINUITY FOR WONDER BREAD

"And Dad will love Wonder Bread's delicious flavor too. Remember it's Wonder Bread for the breast in bed."

SCIENCE PROGRAM

On *Exploring The Unknown*, a science program, Andre Baruch, reading a commercial for a large corporation called it "the largest producers in the United States of Magnoosium, Alleeminum, and Stool."

PRESIDENTIAL SPEECH

HARRY VON ZELL: "Ladies and Gentlemen, the President of the United States, Hoobert Heever."

ELECTRIC SHAVER COMMERCIAL

"Men, when it's time to shave, you have a date with our two-headed model."

THIS IS NEW YORK

Bill Leonard, MC of his own program on CBS called *This Is New York*, in his introduction of Joe E. Brown, neatly said—"Meet Joe E. Brown, currently starving in Harvey."

ANNOUNCER: "This is Indiana's first broad-chasing station."

SAD TALE

Bud Collyer, popular radio and television master of ceremonies, relates the one about one of radio's best known news commentators. The newscaster hadn't gone over his news material in advance this particular evening. He was reading a news item about a prize winning dog who had been crated and shipped from one city to another. It seemed that the valued dog got his tail caught in the crate. The tail apparently was removed, and the irate owner sued for $10,000 in damages. The commentator unhesitatingly said: "That's a lot of money for a piece of tail."

There was a moment of silence while he mulled that one over.

MR. KEENE TRACER OF LOST PERSONS

ANNOUNCER: "We now bring you 'Mister Keene, loser of traced persons.'"

LOCAL NEWS

A local news announcer reported on an accident that befell a citizen of the town while he was making griddle cakes. "Jones' hand was burned when he laid it on a hot girdle."

WAR BOND RALLY

When Walter Pidgeon appeared for a local bond drive, he was greeted by the president of the Drive, who was thrilled at the thought of meeting a movie star. The result of his excitement was the following: "Mr. Privilege, this is indeed a pigeon."

TALL STORY

QUIZMASTER: "What is the Taj Mahal?"
CONTESTANT: (*After hemming and hawing*) "Im afraid I don't know."
QUIZMASTER: "I'm awfully sorry, but you should know that the Taj Mahal, located in India, is the greatest erection man has ever had for woman since time immemorial."

MERRY CHRISTMAS

ANNOUNCER: "And now to conclude our program of Christmas Carols, our guest star will sing 'Come All Ye Faithful,' by Adeste Fidelis."

14

HEARD ON BBC IN ENGLAND

ANNOUNCER: "This is the British Broadcasting Corporation. The next program comes to you from the bathroom at Pump; pardon me, I mean the Pumproom at Bath."

NBC TELEVISION

Eloise McElhone introduced Ham Fisher, celebrated cartoonist, thusly: "And as Anchor Man on our panel tonite, we have the nation's number one cartoonist, Ham Pisher, creator of Joe Falooka."

HOME ECONOMICS PROGRAM

Tommy Dixon, announcer of *Quiz of Two Cities*, remembers a home economics program he was emceeing for KHJ with Norma Young, and the phrase was "Cracked Crab Salad." Three times it came out "crapped crap salad." He finally had to serve lettuce and tomatoes and let it go at that.

COMMERCIAL ANNOUNCEMENT

ANNOUNCER: "Ladies, does your husband wake up in the morning feeling lustless, er, listless?"

RADIO CITY ANNOUNCER

Here's what comes of making poor hard-working announcers get up early in the morning. It happened in the days when the National Broadcasting Company was comprised of the Red Network and the Blue Network (now the American Broadcasting Company). Their facilities were combined in Radio City, New York. One morning, a bleary-eyed announcer dashed into the studio just as he was to deliver his station break. Pressing the monitor button, he declared to the world, "This is either the Red Network or the Blue Network of the National Broadcasting Company."

WORLD NEWS ROUNDUP

COMMENTATOR: "All the world was thrilled with the marriage of the Duck and Doochess of Windsor."

An engineer accidentally threw a switch that cut off the local program and substituted the current network show.

"It's time now, ladies and gentlemen, for our featured guest, the prominent lecturer and social leader, Mrs. Elma Dodge..." (*Superman cut in*) "... who is able to leap tall buildings in a single bound. *SWISHHHH!*"

ELEVEN O'CLOCK NEWS

"was phemoamal ... pheomelel ... phenelemen ... oh heck ... extraordinary!"

MUSICAL QUIZ PROGRAM

During a panel discussion on music, Dr. Sigmund Spaeth, noted tune detective and musicologist, was asked by a student:

QUESTION: "Why is it I'm always enthusiastic about the music of Johann Strauss and always sleep with Aida?"

STOCK ANSWER

ANNOUNCER: "Remember that bulk is important to the digestive tract to aid in regular movement. Mother should have a good stock of Kellogg's Pep so that you can have a bowl every morning. Yes, kids, be sure Mother is stopped up with Kellogg's Pep."

HITS, RUNS AND ERRORS

ANNOUNCER: "We now bring you Dodgers and Hammerstein hits."

CONGRATULATIONS

A disc jockey with good intentions wanted to give a buddy of his a plug on his impending marriage. He innocently said: "I'm going to dedicate our next recording to my pal Henry and his expectant bride."

UNCLE DON'S CHILDREN'S PROGRAM

One lesson an announcer learns is to make sure he is off the air before he makes any private comments. But even the greatest sometimes slip. A legend is Uncle Don's remark after he had closed his famous children's program. He thought his mike was cut off the air when he said, "I guess that will hold the little bastards."

"And just received is a new stock of Reis Sanforized Sport Shirts for men with 15 or 17 necks."

MUSIC QUIZ

Harry Salter, veteran band leader of *Stop the Music* and *Name that Tune* fame, tells about the lady contestant who was asked to identify a popular tune which happened to be "Flat Foot Floogie." The emcee of the program tried every which way to give the contestant a hint as to the correct answer. He said, "If you walked the street all day, what would happen?" "Oh, I know," the lady happily snapped back, "I'd be a Flat Foot Floosie!"

SPIRITUAL?

ANNOUNCER: "Yes, there is no doubt that Stephen Foster was one of the greatest, if not the greatest writer of American folk music. His spirituals rank high among the music the world likes best. And now, Stephen Foster's immortal song, 'Old Jack Blow.'"

JOHN J. ANTHONY HOUR

"Mr. Anthony, I have a problem. My husband isn't talking to me or having anything to do with me since his business fell off."

ARMY INTELLIGENCE

NEWSCASTER: "General Omar Bradley arrived at the conference . . . tall, dignified and uninformed! (*uniformed*)

TEXAS ANNOUNCER

A hillbilly singer, Cecil Gill, was scheduled to sing, "There's An Empty Cot in the Bunk House Tonight." The announcer fluffed "Cecil Gill, the Yodeling Country Boy, will now sing, 'There's An Empty Bunk in the Cathouse Tonight.'"

MISS U.S. TELEVISION CONTEST—NBC-TV

SKITCH HENDERSON: "And now parading before us is a lovely beverage of booties—I beg your pardon, bevy of beauties."

22

SIR STAFFORD CRIPPS

LOWELL THOMAS: "This report is credited to the president of the British Board of Trade, Sir Stifford Crapps."

DISC JOCKEY

There's a young disc jockey who may never live this down. He was spinning up some rock 'n' roll platters. His next recording was "Sunny Side of the Street," which he planned to introduce by saying, "Here's a knocked out version by a new group of 'On the Sunny Side of the Street.'" Instead, this came out over the ether: "And here's a knocked up virgin by a new group."

TV ANNOUNCER

"Our *Late Show* film presentation for this evening will be a revival, featuring the late Leslie Howard as The Scarlet Pumpernickel, er . . . the Scarlet Pimple, I mean, Scarlet Pimpernel."

COMMERCIAL CONTINUITY FOR SCHULTZ'S STORES

ANNOUNCER: "Schultz's Store specializes in courteous, prompt, and efficient self-service."

REQUEST PROGRAM

This was one of those times when the announcer thought the mike was off. This guy, during a particularly bad cold epidemic, had to fill in on the board although he should have stood in bed himself. After he cut off the mike switch and put on a musical recording, someone asked him how he felt. He said, "I feel like hell, and I'm full of Anacin." A few minutes later the phone rang, and a fan requested that he repeat that recording, "I Feel Like Hell, and I'm Full of Anacin."

FILL 'ER UP

When Ed Wynn was the Texaco Fire Chief, Graham McNamee, one of the truly great announcers of all time, did the commercial for Texaco. Ed Wynn kidded Graham for weeks after McNamee reminded his million of listeners, "When you see the famous sign of the Fire Chief, fill up with Texagoo gasaloon."

When a network was doing a series of classic romances, one of radio's most dependable announcers said, "And so ends another virgin of a famous love story."

JOHN REED KING

John Reed King, instead of saying "Lindsay-Crouse play *Life With Father,* spurted out, "That long run Crindsay-Louse play, *Lice With Father.*"

GIVE THE DEVIL HIS DUE

"Stay tuned to a sermon by Reverend Smith. Don't miss it if you can."

SO YOU THINK YOU KNOW MUSIC

On *So You Think You Know Music?*, a musical quiz program on CBS emceed by Ted Cott, a contestant was asked to identify a recorded musical composition. He answered, "It sounds like Smetana's Buttered Bride . . . er . . . I mean . . . Battered Bride, oh the hell with it."

OPEN MIKE

Arlene Francis, popular femcee and panelist on *What's My Line?* was doing a studio audience warmup on *What's My Name,* on radio many years ago. She miscalculated her allotted warmup time and said: "There are thirty seconds to go, if anyone has to." This advice was heard by millions of her listeners.

WALKIE TALKIE

A famous novelist will always remember this fluff. She was narrating one of her programs which had a character, Cybelle, a sleep-walker. The line that went out over the air, however, was "Cybelle was an inveterate street-walker."

COMMERCIAL FOR RUPPERT'S BEER

"When you want to relax after a hard day's work, try Buppert's Rear."

ANNOUNCER: "Ladies, at Zimmer's you will find sneakers that are also excellent for street walking."

28

STAY TUNED

ANNOUNCER: "The following prescribe is transcrammed."

SMOKE-FILLED ROOM

John Daly was chairman of a series of war debates between Senator Taft and ex-representative T. V. Smith. The discussion between the two waxed hot as the broadcast ended, and Daly said, "Senator Taft and Representative Spit smoked from the CBS studios in Washington."

MAGGI McNELLIS

When Maggi McNellis was WEAF's *Column-Miss of the Air,* she set herself a stumbling block when she told of a visit to Ruby Foo's Chinese Restaurant. She began: "A Foo nights ago, at Ruby Few's. . . !"

MILTON CROSS, OPERA SERIES

"NBC now brings you excerpts from the Pill of Princeton ... I beg your pardon, from the Prince of Pilsen."

THE EYES OF TEXAS

Robert Merrill, celebrated baritone of the Metropolitan Opera, said on NBC, "I salute the wen and mimmen of Texas."

NEWS ANNOUNCER

This tongue twister almost cost an announcer his job:

He was describing an air battle during the war. He ended his commentary, "And there, after crashing to the earth, piled in a heap, was a Messerschmitt."

STEVE ALLEN

Steve Allen, popular network radio and TV personality, in an interview once plugged his new show *Songs for Sale* on CBS thusly:

"I think you will like our new sow, Shlongs for Sale."

COMMERCIAL CONTINUITY FOR MRS. WOOLER'S TAILOR SHOP

"For all your needs, remember to visit Mrs. Wooler's Tail Shop."

BURL IVES

Burl Ives upon receiving a scroll from Billboard, presented by Russel Crouse, said: "I want to thank Mr. Brussel Rouse for his screwl."

SPOT QUESTION

"Why didn't you go to school, sonny?"
"Oh, I have the measles."

QUICK ON THE WITHDRAW

XYZ Department Store has in stock an excellent supply of lovely two-place pee suits with zippers.

AUDIENCE PARTICIPATION PROGRAM

FEMCEE: "What are you going to do with all that money, sailor?"
CONTESTANT: "Boy, with all this dough, I am going to do the town."
FEMCEE: "With all this money, the girls will be laying for you tonight."

(*Calgery Rug and Drape Shop program*)
ANNOUNCER: The Calgery Drug and Rape Shop is on the air."

GOOD WILL HOUR

Sometimes participants on a Good Will Hour try to use fifty dollar words and don't quite make it. One attempt to use the word "castigate" resulted in the statement, "I found I had to castrate my father."

REMOTE BAND ANNOUNCER

"You are listening to the mucous of Clyde Lucas."

GALA OPENING

At the opening of a new opera season a local radio station carried the opening night festivities. The female announcer described the arrival of the dignitaries, what they were wearing, etc. She described the entrance of a famous prima donna in this fashion:

"As the house lights are being dimmed, I can see Madame ——————— entering her box, she is now picking her seat."

DICTION AWARD WINNER

DAVID ROSS: "And now we present that great Mexican singing star, Tito Guitar, and his guizar."

RECORD SESSION

DISC JOCKEY: "Stay tuned to that outstanding quartet of the airwaves, bringing you 15 minutes of recorded music. Ladies and Gentlemen, the Stinkpots! er, Inkspots."

BROADWAY CAMERA INTERVIEW WITH TOMMY MANVILLE

GARDNER: "Tommy, you've been married 8 or 9 times. How do you recognize your wives?"

MANVILLE: "Oh, I remember them by the parts I like best!"

WEATHER REPORTER: "... and from the airport's weather bureau we learned that a southeast girl with a wind velocity of seventy miles per hour is reported on her way."

LONG MAY SHE WAVE

On a children's program, a youngster was called upon to recite the Pledge of Allegiance. He stood up, cleared his throat, and this was the result:

"I pledge allegiance to the flag of the United States of America, and to the Republic for Richard Sands; One nation in a dirigible, with Liberty and Justice for all."

COMMERCIAL ANNOUNCEMENT

ANNOUNCER: "At Moe's Esso Station, you can get gassed, charged up, and your parts lubricated in 30 minutes!"

HAPPY NEW YEAR

On New Year's Eve, an announcer who perhaps had one too many, spilled out the following: "This is WJZ, New York. No other station can make that statement."

ALL BALLED UP

Hugh James, veteran NBC announcer, was announcing a program from the Republican National Convention in Philadelphia in 1948. He told of various important balls relating to convention festivities. He reminded his audience to purchase tickets, and gave the location for the purchase of tickets for several balls which were being held during convention week. Upon conclusion he said, "We will now switch you to our studio where the orchestra is now playing the 'Blue Balls of Scotland.'"

⚜ ⚜ ⚜

OH POPPYCOCK

"Oh pappy cack, puppy cock, peppy cook ... oh, nuts!"

⚜ ⚜ ⚜

THIS IS YOUR LIFE

On *This Is Your Life,* exciting human interest program emceed by Ralph Edwards, Lily Pons, celebrated French soprano, was the honored guest. She was flabbergasted at seeing her mother who had arrived unannounced from the east. The program had a tie-in with TWA Airlines, whereby surprise guests were flown in from all over the world. Lily asked her mother, "Mama, did you fly ze airplane?" Her mother replied, "Poof, I took ze train."

A NOSE FOR NUDES

A newscaster came to the studio with a bad cold, with this result:

"Dis is your Prudential reporder bringing you up to da minute nudes."

❖ ❖ ❖

DISC JOCKEY INTERVIEW

Bill Silbert, WMGM disc jockey, interviewed a lady guest. She told Silbert that she had children aged two, three, five and six. Bill smilingly asked, "What happened to four?" The lady snapped back, "Oh, that's the year we got our television set."

❖ ❖ ❖

SO SOLLY

COMMENTATOR: "And what American can ever forget the Jap's infamous attack on Bar Harbor."

BETTY FURNESS

Betty Furness, doing a Westinghouse commercial on an NBC TV program, produced by Kermit Schafer, gave out with this advice: "Try your Westinghoushe waser with a full load on."

❖ ❖ ❖

HISTORICAL REMARK

"This is WNYC New York. You now hear the chimes of hysterical New York."

❖ ❖ ❖

STATION BREAK

"Stay tuned for *I Love Lucly*."

❖ ❖ ❖

BEST MAN

On *Queen for a Day* an eight-year-old boy wanted a new suit. "Why?" the emcee asked. "I wanna wear it tomorrow when my mother and father get married."

ANNOUNCER: "Steinberg's Department Store has just received a shipment of large size bathing suits. Ladies, now you can buy a bathing suit for a ridiculous figure."

GIVE THE LADY $64!

On *Two for the Money*, popular quiz program sponsored by a cigarette company, Herb Shriner, the Indiana Hoosier, asked a contestant, "Are you a natural born citizen of the United States?" "Oh no," the woman replied, "I was born a Caesarean."

⁂

GRAND OPENING

Andre Baruch, veteran announcer and now a sportscaster, recently opened a network radio program in this fashion: "Good ladies, evening and gentlemen of the audio radiancy."

⁂

BROTHER IRA

DISC JOCKEY: Now we hear one of my favorite selections by George Gershwin, with lyrics by his lovely wife, Ira.

I'VE GOT A SECRET

Art Linkletter has learned that children don't have many secrets. Just to make conversation, he recently asked a little girl what her mother had told her not to do that day. "She told me not to announce that she was pregnant," said the child.

❧ ❧ ❧

HOPALONG MOLOTOV

Wild Bill Hickok had his program interrupted by a newscaster just after four shots were fired by the program's sound effects man. "We interrupt this program to bring you a bulletin from the Mutual News Room. L. P. Beria has just been executed, according to an announcement from Moscow Radio. We now return you to *Wild Bill Hickok*." At that moment, Guy Madison was reading this line: "Well, that should hold him for a while."

❧ ❧ ❧

BOY ANNOUNCER

COMMERCIAL: "I have been using Pepsodent since I was a little boy. My mother and father have been using Pepsodent since they were little boys."

"Final results of the FFA contest are: Apple picking won by Dick Jones. Tractor driving award to Jack Davis. One of our own girls, Miss Betty Smith, was chosen as the best hoer."

GOOD ADVICE

ANNOUNCER: Try this lovely four-piece starter set in your home for seven days. If you are not satisfied, return it to us. So you see you have everything to lose and nothing to gain.

❖ ❖ ❖

MYRT AND MARGE

One of the principal characters on *Myrt and Marge* was Myrtle Hayfield, until an actor came out with "You're just a feel, Myrtle Hayfool."

❖ ❖ ❖

GOOD NIGHT!

Performers on all-night telethons get very tired. A perfect example is Morey Amsterdam's appearance on one of these marathons for a worthy cause. Here is what came out, at approximately 3 o'clock in the morning. "Mr. and Mrs. Geilgud of the Bronx sent $2.00. And here's another contribution of $2.00 if you will tell Theresa to go to bed." "All right, Theresa will go to bed for $2.00."

HERBERT'S COUSIN

Durwood Kirby, on the Garry Moore show, said: "Ladies, I have here a heever clooner."

❖ ❖ ❖

CAN-CAN

ANNOUNCER: "Mrs. Manning's are the finest pork and beans you ever ate.... So when you order pork and beans, be sure Mrs. Manning is on the can."

❖ ❖ ❖

THEY'LL LOVE IT IN BOSTON

The following was heard on Arthur Godfrey's *Talent Scouts*. "I'm not going to read the Kinsey book, I'm going to wait 'til they make it into a movie."

❖ ❖ ❖

WOR LATE NEWS COVERAGE

"And now here's the full story on the Russian freighter that *crapsized* in Portland's harbor this afternoon."

WASH DAY

ANNOUNCER: When you try Phillips Dental Magnesia, you will find that it makes an excellent mouse wash.

❖ ❖ ❖

A BAD SPELL OF WEATHER

Another classic blooper was contributed by the distinguished Frank Knight: "And here is the weather report, tomorrow roudy followed by clain!"

❖ ❖ ❖

MUSICAL PIECE

ANNOUNCER: "And now our pianist is going to tear off a piece named *Margie*."

❖ ❖ ❖

MIGHTY MOUSE

Jack Stilwell of WLS Chicago tells of an announcer doing a commercial for rodenticide: "When you use this rodent killer all mats and rice will immediately disappear."

BEHIND THE MIKE

On a *Man on the Street* interview on a radio station in Kansas City, Missouri, the announcer stopped for a sidewalk interview with a farmer, who was standing next to his donkey.

"What is your name, sir?" asked the emcee.

"Elmer Brown," replied the farmer.

"And where are you from?"

"I'm from St. Jo," he drawled.

"Isn't that at least 50 miles from here?"

"Yes sir, 'tis."

"Tell me, what are you doing in the middle of all this traffic?"

"Jest restin' my ass."

❖ ❖ ❖

NBC NATIONAL BISCUIT COMPANY

Bill Garden, Director of Special Events at NBC-TV, recalls an announcer who hurriedly finished a religious program to be in time for a station break. He closed by saying, "Cast thy broad upon the waters." He couldn't finish the quotation in time so he concluded with, "This is the National Breadcasting Company."

(*Laundromat commercial*)

ANNOUNCER: "Ladies who care to drive by and drop off their clothes will receive prompt attention."

PLAYING POSSUM

On a favorite soap opera, an actor came out with this classic: "Look out, boys, here comes the sheriff with his possum."

※ ※ ※

YOU CAN BE SURE IF IT'S WESTINGHOUSE

On *What's My Line?* over the CBS network, a panel tries to guess the visitors' occupations, and at each show a celebrity appears as a "mystery guest." On a recent program, film actress Marilyn Maxwell was answering questions which were to elicit only yes or no replies. One panel member queried, "Are you female?" Miss Maxwell gave a slightly longer answer: "I was, last time I looked."

※ ※ ※

SOME CHOKE

At WLW, Cincinnati, they are still giggling over the announcer who, in cathedral tones, urged his audience to buy "Viceroys—if you want a good choke."

PUNCH LINE

An announcer, following the Herring-Gambio fight on TV, reminded his listeners: "Remember every Friday night is fright night on NBC."

❖ ❖ ❖

KNIFE, FORK AND SPOONERISM

A CBS performer gave these directions for setting a table: "Place the sports and foons on the . . ." Then he tried it once more: "I mean the sporks and sphoons . . . !" Then he tried it a third time: "Of course I mean the porks and soons."

❖ ❖ ❖

HAPPY BIRTHDAY

Johnny Olsen, popular Quizmaster and Master of Ceremonies interviewed a contestant on *Whiz Quiz*, an audience participation program on ABC. The contestant, a 90-year-old sea captain, was celebrating his birthday.

OLSEN: "Well, captain, how does it feel to be 90 years old?"
CAPTAIN: "Top side, I'm all right, but below the water line, I ain't worth a damn."

Act It Out!

A NEW WORD INVENTED

Walter Rainey, Dumont Television news commentator, gave out with this classic:

"Here is a news item about the Russians that once again crapped up in the news."

❖ ❖ ❖

DAVE GARROWAY

On an NBC Program, Dave Garroway, one of TV's cleverest personalities, advised the use of his favorite soap, for your shlub or tower.

❖ ❖ ❖

HEAVY PLANE TRAVEL

On KOA, Denver, a newscaster told his audience, "Rita Hayworth is now reposing on a Nevada Nude Ranch."

❖ ❖ ❖

NEWS BULLETIN

ANNOUNCER: (*excitedly*) "Ladies and Gentlemen, we interrupt this news bulletin to bring you a program."

DEAN OF ANNOUNCERS

MILTON CROSS: "The A&P Program, starring Harry Horlick and his A&G Pippsies."

❖ ❖ ❖

PRIZE REMARK

Just before the prize-fight, the chief announcer at Madison Square Garden wished the two contenders luck, by saying, "May the winner emerge victorious."

❖ ❖ ❖

MOREY AMSTERDAM
CHOCK FULL OF NUTS PROGRAM

In his anxiety to please his new sponsor, on Chock Full of Nuts, on NBC-TV, Morey Amsterdam tripped over the client's name and spurted out you will enjoy a "Jock Full of Nuts Special."

GOOD DEAL

"At Tri-Boro Furniture Store you will find floor coverings, lamps and an occasional piece for any room in the house."

❖ ❖ ❖

JUST PEACHY

An announcer commented as follows in a recent newscast: "Well, we have a new Miss America, a Georgia piece, I mean peach, er, a lady from Georgia."

❖ ❖ ❖

NBC COAST TO COAST SERIAL DRAMA

ACTRESS: "The fog was as thick as seepoop."

❖ ❖ ❖

WORLD NEWS

Bob Denton, in a broadcast introducing Helen Kiett, who was about to broadcast a news show from Spain, said: "NBC now brings you the only woman correspondent in pain. . . ."

A DAY AT THE RACES

In a broadcast originating from Monmouth Race Track in New Jersey, the announcer was making introductory remarks in preparation for the feature race which was to be run in a few minutes. He was running down the entries when he noticed that the horse which was the favorite, named Harass, was not going to run. He reminded the listener to be sure to scratch Harass!

♣ ♣ ♣

WHATS COOKIN'?

On a cooking show which originated from a Philadelphia station, a housewife told of a delightful new way "to prepare fricken chicasee."

♣ ♣ ♣

OUT IN FRONT

In an interview on a Toronto television program, a woman guest was asked, "Isn't it true that you have been named one of the ten best-breasted women in Canada?"

ANNOUNCER: "At Heitman's you will find a variety of fine foods, expertly served by experienced waitresses in appetizing forms."

I REMEMBER MAMA

COMMERCIAL: "Give this lovely Cannon Towel set to either your sister, aunt, niece, or mother as a wedding present."

❖ ❖ ❖

UNDERCOVER MAN

On *Date in Manhattan,* on NBC-TV, an announcer was describing a multi-colored reversible blanket in this fashion, "When you are in bed, and you get tired of 'er on one side, just turn 'er over."

❖ ❖ ❖

BOB DENTON, VETERAN ABC ANNOUNCER

"The following pewgram of Moosic comes to you from Radio City."

HONESTY IS THE BEST POLICY

The TV play was *Abe Lincoln in Illinois* . . . in which Raymond Massey starred. The actors on stage were bidding farewell to the president. . . . When one of them called out . . . "G'bye Mister Massey."

❖ ❖ ❖

ANNOUNCER IN THE GROOVE

A welcome relief in an announcer's day comes when a program is transcribed. On Sunday mornings, a staff member of a small western station would set a transcribed sermon on the turntable and then run out for a cup of coffee. He had the procedure timed perfectly: he was always back in time to set up the second half of this half-hour sermon. One Sunday he returned to the unattended control room to find the telephone ringing madly. The needle had caught in the groove of a record, early in the program, and for fifteen minutes came the words. "Go to hell, go to hell, go to hell."

❖ ❖ ❖

WHAT'S COOKIN'?

"Tune in tomorrow and find out if John will goose Sadie's cook, er I mean, will John cook Sadie's goose?"

(*Dinah Shore show*)
"Good evening, ladies and gentlemen, it's time for songs —so welcome to the Dinasaur Show!"

NEWS PROGRAM SPONSORED BY SCOTCH SOAP

NEWSCASTER: "Again—Scotch Soup covers the nose."

❖ ❖ ❖

ROYAL WELCOME

From Bennett Cerf comes the fluff credited to a Washington commentator covering the visit of England's King and Queen.

COMMENTATOR: "When they arrive you will hear a
(*gravely*)   twenty-one son galute."

❖ ❖ ❖

ARTHUR GODFREY

The fabulous Arthur Godfrey doing a Lipton Tea commercial on CBS said, "When you are through with your old bag, just discard her, er, I mean, it."

❖ ❖ ❖

COMMERCIAL

ANNOUNCER: "Don't forget to visit your A and Poo Feed Store."

TASTY SNACKS

ANNOUNCER: "For a sizzling snake and pasty snack, remember the Fraser Cafe."

※ ※ ※

QUIZ PROGRAM

A contestant on a quiz program was asked, "What do you find on pool tables that you find in men's trousers?"

The answer should have been pockets.

※ ※ ※

HONORABLE MISTAKE

After the bombing of Pearl Harbor, an announcer, extremely angry, shouted:

"Everybody today would like to take a crap at the Japs —er, I mean—take a crack at the Japs."

COLONEL STOOPNAGLE STUMP CLUB QUIZ

STOOPNAGLE: "And what do you do for a living, my good lady?"
LADY: "I'm a maid. I do housework, and take care of a large family."
STOOPNAGLE: "How large a family?"
LADY: "Well, let's see, there are four boys, three girls, one adult, and one adultress."

⚜ ⚜ ⚜

THE BIG PAYOFF

Bess Meyerson, former Miss America, and co-MC on *The Big Payoff*, popular network TV program, was interviewing a contestant on the program. She was handed a note from one of the members of the production staff, which told her that the contestant was London bound, so as to get this added color into her interview. Believing that this note was an added reminder of the contestant's name, she introduced him thusly: "Ladies and gentlemen, I would like you to meet Mr. London Bound."

JONES AND HARE

JONES: "Did you hear, I just bought a new car?"
HARE: "What kind of car?"
JONES: "I don't remember, but I know it starts with P."
HARE: "Don't kid me, no car starts with P."

❖ ❖ ❖

JACK ARMSTRONG PROMOTION

An announcer plugging network programs advised his audience to be sure and listen to that model American youth, typifying the best in boyhood, "Jerk Armstrong, all-American boy."

❖ ❖ ❖

MADISON SQUARE GARDEN

"It's a hot night at the Garden, folks, and at ringside I see several ladies in gownless evening straps."

"We promise you the most exciting trip of your life—just imagine those perfect days under bright skies, on white coral sands. This is the best time of the year for Bermuda—so when you fly, be sure to take a plane."

NEXT?

Eddie Peabody, the great banjoist, was introduced thusly:

ANNOUNCER: "Ladies and Gentlemen: Mr. Eddie Playbody will now pee for you."

❖ ❖ ❖

SILENCE IS GOLDEN

"What did you have for breakfast, son?"
(complete silence)
"What did you have for breakfast, son?"
(complete silence)
"Daddy, you're hurting my arm."

❖ ❖ ❖

GOING, GOING, GONE

For a small cash payment at the Smiling Irishman used car lot, you will be guaranteed secondhand automobiles in first-crash condition.

GIRLS WILL BE GIRLS

Ina Ray Hutton, on her NBC-TV show featuring her all girl orchestra, told her audience: "Our girls like booze in any form—pardon me, that should be blues."

※ ※ ※

HANG IT, ANYWAY

"Try Slenderella and you can use a few lynches. I'm sorry, that should be lose a few lynches."

※ ※ ※

BEGORRA!

Here's a question from *Double or Nothing*, CBS, that rocked the studio audience with laughter:

QUESTION: Where is the Orange Free State?
ANSWER: California! I mean Florida!

※ ※ ※

A NEAT TRICK

Dick Kollmar, on the *Dorothy and Dick* breakfast program, blooped, "If Pasteur was alive, he would turn over in his grave."

(Commercial for Bernard Men's Clothing Store)
"You will always find the best dressed men at Barnyards."

LESSON IN PRONUNCIATION

There are some confusing words in this language of ours, for example "brazier", spelled b-r-a-z-i-e-r, meaning a holder for hot coals. But that isn't the way this announcer saw it.

"And the last memo, ladies, from your radio shopping service, is a Father's Day reminder. It's barbecue time and Schmidt's Hardware at 234 Main Street, at the corner of Maple, is featuring an ideal gift for Dad on his special day. An all-purpose brassiere for delicious outdoor meals."

❖ ❖ ❖

BEAR WITH IT

On *Share the Wealth,* popular radio quiz program, contestants were asked to name several events in history associated with animals, such as the horse in Paul Revere's ride. When the quizmaster came to Lady Godiva, a young lady contestant unhesitatingly answered *"Bear!"*

❖ ❖ ❖

FINAL WARNING

"This is a final warning! Failure to report to your alien officer may result in your deportation or prostitution!"

HELP!

(*News Program*) "Down in Washington the legal tangle got to be just too hot for the teamster's boss unionman. According to latest reports received here, Dave Beck has just sent for his liar."

⚜ ⚜ ⚜

NOTE

"And from Cheyenne comes word that the 34th Wyoming State Legislature is in its final week of law breaking!"

⚜ ⚜ ⚜

HASTE MAKES WASTE

The one thing in radio and television that never changes is time. The clock on the wall won't wait for anybody. You have to start your show on time and finish on time. When you are running late, things like this are bound to happen.

"It's a nine pound boy born at Memorial Hospital for Mr. and Mrs. Jack Jason of Elm Road. Mrs. Jason was the former Susan Mulhaney. Services will be held tomorrow at 2 P.M. at Morton's Funeral Chapel for Jasper Howard, age 91, who passed on in his sleep yesterday. I'm sorry, our time is running out, so several deaths and births will have to be postponed until next week at the same time."

SWORN TO BE GOOD

Heard on the Klavin and Finch Disc Jockey Show, WNEW, New York:

"You'll hear about these wonderful cupcakes during the curse of the next commercial!"

❖ ❖ ❖

THE PAWS THAT REFRESHES

Poor timing and improper pauses can be the source of many a headache for announcers, as evidenced by the improper change of pace.

". . . And the United Nations will adjourn until next week. And now here's a local news item: A lot of villagers were very startled today when a pack of dogs broke loose from a dog catcher's wagon and raced crazily through the fields of a well known tobacco plantation. . . . Friends, does your cigarette taste different lately?"

❖ ❖ ❖

MACARONI, ANYONE?

Heard on the coast-to-coast network show, *Young Dr. Malone:*

"Nurse, be sure to give the patient a hypodemic noodle!"

A LICENSED VET?

On one of the nation's most popular day time soap operas, an actor had a line to read where he was supposed to say, "Let's give the bell a pull." He read it: "Let's give the bull a pill."

✣ ✣ ✣

HEAT SNAP

WEATHER FORECASTER: "The Mid West is suffering from one of the worst cold-spells in years, with temperatures dropping as low as twenty degrees below zero. Tomorrow's forecast is for continued mild!"

✣ ✣ ✣

THREE FOR THE PRICE OF ONE

On an Arkansas station, a selection of hillbilly records were apparently mixed with a shipment of classical records, with the following result:

"Now here's an interesting looking record—it's got a classical label, sung by a trio, John, Charles and Thomas."

"Good afternoon, this is your department store TV counselor—Here's news for those who have little time for your Christmas shopping. Tonight, after working hours on the sixth floor, models will display gowns half off."

NEW HORIZONS

This incident occurred on the *College of Musical Knowledge,* widely-heard musical and audience participation program. The MC was surprised that a lady contestant, young in appearance, had nine children. He asked what her husband did.

"Oh! my husband operates an automatic screwing machine!"

❖ ❖ ❖

BY GEORGE . . .

"Ladies and gentlemen, we regret that due to circumstances beyond our control we are unable to bring you the baseball game from Wrigley Field, so, due to a mistake, we bring you Liberace!"

❖ ❖ ❖

LOVE IS A MANY SPLENDORED THING

"And from Mexico City comes word that Patty McCormick, the American female bullfighter, is resting comfortably in a hospital after being gored by an infatuated bull."

ABIE'S IRISH ROSE

A recent mayor of New York City was guest of honor at a banquet tendered to him by some fellow Irish-Americans. Here is the way the MC introduced His Honor.

"Ladies and Gentlemen, our guest of honor today, is a man you all know. He started as a policeman on the force in harness, rose to a captain of detectives and today occupies a position of great eminence in our city. It's my pleasure at this time to introduce to you His Honor, Myer O'Dwyer!"

♣ ♣ ♣

STATION BREAK

"This is KTIW, Sexas Titty er, Texas City."

♣ ♣ ♣

HOME CARE

TV pitchmen talk fast and sometimes talk themselves into trouble, as for example:

"A worn out rug can spoil the appearance of a beautiful home, but here's what you can do to correct the situation. Just send a postal card addressed to Rugs, Rugs c/o this station, and we will have our expert come into your home to examine your worn-out piles."

ANNOUNCER: "Stay tuned for Roy Neal and his program of music for your every nude."

OOPS!

"You are tuned to WOKO, Albany's worst station!"

❖ ❖ ❖

CHILLING MOMENT

A young lady pinch-hitting for Betty Furness was unfamiliar with the equipment she was demonstrating. Here was the result.

"There's no reason to be satisfied with old-styled refrigerators. This Westinghouse is completely automatic—a self defrosting feature takes care of that. Let's look inside—just the slightest push on this snap-open door and uh! wait a minute—just push—wait a minute. Oh, this opens—I guess you'll just have to take my word for it."

❖ ❖ ❖

SPECIAL OFFER

"Friday is poultry night—remember all ladies present will get a free goose. That is, all ladies will get a goose for free."

HOW'S THAT AGAIN?

"Well let's spin another disk. This time it's Jose Ferrar's recent bride, Harry James, with Rosemary Clooney on the trumpet."

※ ※ ※

HEARD YOU THE FIRST TIME

"Stay tuned now for a dramatization of Dickens' immortal *Sale of Two Titties*. UH! I mean *Tale of Two Cities*."

※ ※ ※

NO COMMENT

In the dictionary you will find a word spelled P-A-E-A-N and pronounced pē'ăn. It means to praise. However, an ice-cream sponsor didn't endorse this announcer's choice of words.

"And now is a good time to paean Brody's ice cream."

PASS THE BICARB

On *Two For The Money*, popular TV program, a young lady was asked about her occupation.

"I work for the Pittsburgh Natural Gas Company. Over ninety percent of the people in Pittsburgh have gas!"

♣ ♣ ♣

FORWARD, MARCH

"The American League standings show the Cleveland Indians in first place with the New York Yankees close up there behind."

♣ ♣ ♣

THAT'S SERVICE

"Remember, for excellence in service, take your car to your local Ford dealer. Every car after being serviced is test-driven by the mechanics. See what a bang up job he can do."

♣ ♣ ♣

STILL NO COMMENT

"On his recent visit to the United States Emperor Haile Selassie of Ethiopia made an eloquent pee for peace."

ONE MAN'S MEAT

When a station carries two programs, one local and one network, the crossing of the two lines can bring unexpected effects. Listen to this:

"The recipe this afternoon is for potato pancakes. I'm sure you will enjoy them. You take six medium sized potatoes, deep fat . . . and I am sure your guests will just love them. *(Cut in)* Funeral services will be held promptly at two o'clock."

❖ ❖ ❖

GEOGRAPHY LESSON

Here's an incident from a *Man on the Street* quiz show:

EMCEE: "Now, Mr. Esposito, are you ready for your second question?"
MR. ESPOSITO: "That's a right."
EMCEE: "Your category is bodies of water. Will you tell me—where would you find the Great Lakes?"
MR. ESPOSITO: "The Great a Lakes? uppa U. S.!"

❖ ❖ ❖

SPECIAL DISH

"So . . . for a heavenly Italian dinner, that your entire family will enjoy, try Chef Boy-ar-dee Mariwanna Sauce."

MINISTER: "Don't forget next week's sermon entitled, 'Do you know what hell is?'—Come in and hear our organist."

TASTY BUT PASTY

"Beat the egg yolk and then add the milk, then slowly blend in the sifted flour. As you do you can see how the mixture is sickening. I beg your pardon, I didn't mean sickening I meant thickening" (*Off mike*) "Oh, I goofed there, I know."

❖ ❖ ❖

NEWS OF THE WEEK

"And now, ladies and gentlemen of the radio audience, it gives me great pleasure to introduce you to the Virgin of Governors Island."

❖ ❖ ❖

ATTENTION!

"Stay tuned when, in ten seconds, this station brings you the next installment of Wife's Other John."

❖ ❖ ❖

CALLING ALL CARS

"Your attention please! Your attention please! A little boy has been found lost."

HERE'S THE DIRT

Heard on Hedda Hopper's program:

"Today, one of our well known movie actors traveled incognito to Hot Springs for his annual bath."

❖ ❖ ❖

DOCTOR IN THE HOUSE?

A local 4-H Health Club was being presented with awards by the mayor of the town. In making this presentation, the mayor was reading from a prepared speech that read:

"And now it is with great pleasure that I present this plague to you."

❖ ❖ ❖

GOOD SPORTS

SPORTSCASTER: "The proceeds of the Annual All-Star Game goes to indignant ballplayers—I beg your pardon, that is indigent ballplayers."

❖ ❖ ❖

THANKS A LOT

The following was heard on a local Public Service Program:

"So—don't forget that our mobile X-ray unit will examine you for tuberculosis and other diseases which you will receive free of charges."

"The governor this week is hunting beer, er, I mean bear —well, that is with his clothes on, in the Colorado Mountains."

MUSIC TO SWEAR BY

On a musical quiz program, a twelve-year-old student was asked to identify a classical selection. This was his classic answer ... "I think I know. Is it the Damn Nation of Faust?"

❖ ❖ ❖

NEW INGREDIENT

ANNOUNCER: "Ladies, when you're shopping at the corner grocer's, be sure to stock up on several quarts of Sealtest Ice Cream containing Joy, the wonderful new household detergent."

❖ ❖ ❖

PLEASE OMIT BRICKBATS

Igor Cassini, famous columnist and TV personality, cut a guest star off with the following:

"I'd love to really hear more about your motion picture, but unfortunately, Jane Harvey is going to sing."

WHERE'S EKE?

"And word comes to us from Washington that Ake is indisposed with a stomach ike."

♣ ♣ ♣

ANYWAY, SHE'S BACK

NEWS ANNOUNCER: "A recent arrival back in New York after a stay abroad is the U. S. ambassador to Italy, Miss Clare Loose Booth . . . I beg your pardon . . . that should be Miss Clare Luth Boose."

♣ ♣ ♣

CHARCOAL MAKER

ANNOUNCER: "At the Thrift Stores, with each purchase of a TV Set, you'll receive a brand new toaster that you will appreciate. It automatically burns toast."

TIMBER!

This was a commercial for a housing project:

"Here's a house for sale that won't last long."

♣ ♣ ♣

SCRATCHED

Here is how a Mid-West disc jockey introduced a new recording titled *Lazy Gondolier*.... "Designs in music continues now with Mantovani's most recent recording from London *Lousy Gondolier!*"

♣ ♣ ♣

SEASON'S GREETINGS

In giving an on-the-air promotion during the holiday season, an announcer was reading a Hopalong Cassidy Promotion Spot that came out like this:

"Happy Long Cassidy will be here on Channel 12 at 5:00 P.M. today to wish you a Hoppy New Year!"

DRINK TO ME ONLY

An announcer on WAGA radio in Georgia fluffed a commercial for a popular drink thusly:

"It's a full thirty-two ounces that will serve sex easily."

※ ※ ※

MUSICAL MONEY-MAKERS

A disc jockey had a sentence with one too many t's in it. The result was this description of the latest rage in music:

"Stay tuned tomorrow at two for twenty minutes of Rotten Toll Tunes."

※ ※ ※

QUICK THINKING

Steve Allen was demonstrating the virtues of a non-breakable fibre glass chair on *Tonight* TV show. The manufacturer had told him to take a hammer and strike the chair as hard as he wished. After the first whack, pandemonium broke loose when he poked a hole right through the chair. . . . He bailed himself out by ad libbing: "Well, anyway, this *hammer* is made of fibre glass."

This bit of information leaked through the public address system at Ebbets Field in Brooklyn:

"Ladies, another complaint has been received. Will those of you in the front row boxes kindly remove your clothes?"

TIME SAVER

In Denver, Colo., a laundry commercial was twisted in this manner:

"When your clothing is returned there is little left to iron."

❖ ❖ ❖

MONEY, MONEY

A minister on a Detroit TV Station, asking for donations, looked into the camera and said, "And now, dear funds...."

❖ ❖ ❖

WOW OF A SIGN-OFF

William Dean, when he was giving a sign-off for a 100-watt station in the Dakotas, was heard to say, "This is KABR, Aberdeen, South Dakota, operating on a frequency of 1430 kilocycles with 100 potts of wower!"

STAFF OF LIFE

Jim Mendes, a disc jockey in Providence, Rhode Island, reports this incident on a show that he did:

". . . And now, before we continue with our household hints program, let's have a word about VITAMIN PLUS bread. The next time you visit your corner grocer, be sure to ask for VITAMIN PLUS. You'll love its delicious freshness. Remember, too, that VITAMIN PLUS is double raped."

❖ ❖ ❖

WE WHO DREAM

A student announcer at SMU, worried about her exams, made the following announcement on a musical show:

"And, now, the Concerto in A-Minus."

A sports announcer while giving a play-by-play description of a football game, commented:

"Sam Gary, master of the quick kick, is fading into the end zone for a quick kiss!"

FORE!

On *Name That Tune*, on NBC-TV, a contestant was asked to identify *Hail to the Chief* which was played by the orchestra. MC Bill Cullen tried helping the girl by hinting, "What do they play whenever the President's around?" She answered, "Golf."

❧ ❧ ❧

GAGNET

(*Local Newscast*) "Credit for the discovery of the stolen automobile was given to Lieutenant Blank, a defective of the Los Angeles farce."

❧ ❧ ❧

PATERNITY QUESTION

A daytime news and record show gave rise to this incident on a Denver radio station:

"Before our next recorded selection, here's an item of interest—last night at the Municipal Hospital there were 42 babies born ... and now ... *Don't Blame Me.*"

TOP SECRET

Heard on the eleven o'clock news over NBC:

"Word comes to us from usually reliable White Horse souses."

♣ ♣ ♣

TIME MARCHES ON

An announcer after an exhausting day loaded with commercials, blurted the following:

"It's 9:00 P.M. B-U-L-O-V-A, Bulova Watch Time. This Christmas, buy the new Bulova President; curved to fit the foot!"

♣ ♣ ♣

A WOMAN ALONE

On KALW, San Francisco:

"And now, Nelson Eddy sings *While My Lady Sleeps* with the men's chorus."

THIS IS POLITICS?

On KHBG, Okmulgee, Okla., listeners heard the following:

"Good evening, everyone. This is Bob Vandeventer speaking from the corny count house, where tonight we'll bring you election returns as late as possible."

♣ ♣ ♣

BOTTOM FALLING

Sid Walton, on a coast-to-coast newscast over the Mutual network, said, "The nation was glad to learn that, in the cold of winter, John L. Lewis dropped his union suit."

♣ ♣ ♣

SPIRITED TUNE

On a remote musical program originating from a hotel, an announcer introduced the next musical selection thusly:

"The next selection is dedicated to my girl—*I Don't Stand a Chance with a Ghost Like You!*"

SOLLY, LONG NUMBER

Heard on an early morning disc jockey program that has Extra Long Grain Carolina Rice as a sponsor:

"So, housewives, when you are at your corner grocer, remember to ask for Extra wrong Carolina lice!"

※ ※ ※

NOTHING TRIVIAL, WE HOPE

On a station giving the local news, the following was heard:

"We note with regrettable sorrow that Mrs. Vandermeer is recovering from a bad fall on the ice."

※ ※ ※

THE LAW'S DELAY

A local newscast told of Mrs. Downes, the sheriff's wife, who attended a local flower show with her twin daughters —Anne, age 6, and Alice, age 9.

On a noted news program, the newscaster was heard to say, "Police authorities are finding the solution of murders more and more difficult to solve because the victims are unwilling to cooperate with the police."

ANATOMY LESSON

A Chicago MC and disc jockey introduced a new recording in this fashion:

"And now here is a record all of you rock 'n' roll fans will dig the most—by the popular Pelvis Presley!"

✣ ✣ ✣

BOOMERANG

Igor Cassini, on an NBC television program, threw a cue to the announcer ten minutes too soon. "And now, a word from our announcer . . ." The announcer was totally unprepared and, completely shocked, said, "Hello, ladies and gentlemen—and now back to Igor Cassini."

✣ ✣ ✣

NEATEST TRICK OF THE MONTH

Weather forecast:

"Of the 29 days in February, 126 were clear."

LET US SAY GRACE

Word has been received that Gene Kelly has accepted Prince Rainier's proposal—and now he will become a Princess.

❖ ❖ ❖

WARM PRAISE

On a dramatic program extolling the heroics of a famous World War I hero, an actor referred to the man as a "battle-scared veteran."

❖ ❖ ❖

A WOMAN'S WORLD

On a local society program, presided over by the president of the local women's garden club, the following was heard:

"At the swap shop social held last week, all of our ladies brought something they didn't need. We were happy to see so many members with their husbands."

ANNOUNCER: "This evening, at eleven PM, the Night Owl TV Theatre will present an action-packed tale of adventure starring Gary Cooper in the *"Lives of the Bagel Lancers."*

YES, DO

On the Stork Club program, emceed by Sherman Billingsley, the following was heard:

"Yes, Sherman, I have had a simply delightful, indescribable time here in New York." "That's fine," said Billingsley, "tell us about it."

❖ ❖ ❖

GOOD FRIDAY

"Your Masterwork Concert Hour will now present Boris Godounov, the only opera Mussorgsky ever wrote on Friday evening."

❖ ❖ ❖

FOLLOWED BY MONDAY

WEATHER FORECASTER: "Tomorrow's forecast is mostly Sunday."

INTRODUCING ONCE AGAIN . . .

Blooper history repeated itself when—Chet Huntley, NBC commentator, during the Republican National convention in San Francisco, referred to Herbert Hoover, Jr. as "Heebert Hoover"!

❖ ❖ ❖

BAD LUCK

A sportscaster reported that Sam Snerd seems to have his greatest difficulty playing the Augorsta Golf Curse.

❖ ❖ ❖

SWORN IN

On WMAJ, in Pennsylvania, the following was heard on a newscast:

"Secretary Dulles announces that America has withdrawn her offer to support the Egyptian Aswan Dam. Now it looks as though the only source of funds will be the Soviet Union for the dam project."

NOTHING PERSONAL

During a speech delivered by Emily Kimbrough, prominent writer, the technical equipment became faulty. From out of nowhere a voice was heard stating that "there must be a screw loose in our speaker."

❖ ❖ ❖

HOORAY FOR OUR SIDE

Let's go back to the year 1942 and listen to a war newscast from BBC in England.

"And the Ration Board has announced that in the next few weeks there will be an increase in the allotment of certain food commodities. There is good news on the war front tonight. From North Africa comes word that Allied Troops have stopped the advances of Hitler's Pansy Divisions."

❖ ❖ ❖

DEVILISHLY CLEVER

"Don't forget—tune in tomorrow morning to listen to Phil Cook. He's that clever fellow who plays all voices on his own program. So tomorrow, start your day with laughter. Tune in on Phil Cook, that man with the thousand vices."

FLIGHT PLAN

"Our Airlines has scheduled five flights daily, and you can now fly to Chicago for only $36.00; Los Angeles for $80.00; and we promise you, you will find your plane flight to Miami one of the greatest frights you've ever had."

❖ ❖ ❖

WEATHER EXPERIMENT

"And that's the weather report from the International Airport here at Anchorage, Alaska. Now we'll take a leak out the window to see if it's freezing outside our studio."

❖ ❖ ❖

TWO FOR THE MONEY

"Starting next week at the Paramount Theater you will see that rollicking comedy smash hit *Pale Face*, starring Bob Hope, America's favorite comedian, and lovely Jane Russell. Boy, what a pair!"

"Stay tuned for Phil Spitoonly and his all-ghoul orchestra."

FERRY GOOD NEWS!

"The flood waters in Connecticut are receding. All train service has been re-established. The good weather news for tomorrow is clearing and fair, and here in the Metropolitan area all fairies are operating normally."

※ ※ ※

PARLEZ-VOUS ANGLAIS?

A French Canadian announcer blooped his way through this one.

"This is the Dominion network of the Canadian Broad Corping Castration."

※ ※ ※

LEADING PART

"In ten seconds it will be seven o'clock. Stay tuned for *One Man's Fanny*."

COLORFUL TUNE

"And now here again is that current tit of the day, *Cherry Pink and Assle Blossom White.*"

❖ ❖ ❖

CARRIED AWAY

Sports announcers are human—sometimes even they can be overwhelmed by the excitement of the moment.

(*Noise of crowds*)
"Got twenty-eight seconds to go—there's the snap back from center—looks like a pass—it is a pass."
(*Screams*)
"There he goes—he's up to ten, up to twenty, to thirty— he does it—"
(*Screams*)
"He's going wild, he's going, going—look at that son of a bitch run!"

❖ ❖ ❖

AH, SPRING

"Well, it looks like the end of the cold spell. Spring seems to be on its way. Residents of this area will find relief in the warm ass headed this way. Er . . . that should be warm mass of air headed this way."

Milton Cross, dean of announcers, is responsible for this gem:

"And now stay stewed for the news."

A CHILD CAN DO IT

A television salesman was demonstrating a new do-it-yourself aeroplane kit for youngsters.

"Well, now, you can have this model plane all for yourself, and it's a lot of fun. You just take the kit and it comes completely set up for you. All the parts are ready to put together. You take the part and you well—now you—well, this section here is—well it's—just a minute now. It must be a little stiff and you—this is a very educational toy . . . It teaches children how to cuss!"

❖ ❖ ❖

HAPPENS TO THE BEST OF US

"Well, sorry, folks, we won't be able to spin the rest of that one for you. We seem to be having a little bit of turntable trouble. That record seems to have been broken. That was *My Old Flame* with a crack in her!"

❖ ❖ ❖

GREAT ENTERTAINMENT

"There's excitement in store on our *Million Dollar Movie* tonight with Ann Sheridan—stay tuned as Phillips Milk of Magnesia brings you *Woman on the Run*."

FOR THE CHILDREN

The fabulous Davey Crockett fad was climaxed with this commercial:

"Calling all parents, calling all kids! Here's your chance to buy a Davey Crockett bed—yes, friends, Hunt's Furniture Store has Davey Crockett beds—it's a twin size bed, just right for the kids—with scenes of Davey Crockett in action on the mattress!"

❖ ❖ ❖

TIMELY

Six P.M. Standard Central Time—I meant Central Standard Time. This is your Prudential News reporter bringing you up-to-the-minute news from the wire of U. P. and I. P. Er—I mean I. P. and U. P."

❖ ❖ ❖

HOUSEWIVES, BEWARE!

"So, when you are out shopping, ladies, be sure to look for Dugan Light Diet Bread baked by fresh Dugan Brothers."

FOR MUSIC LOVERS

"Tonight your city station brings you a summertime treat. We take you to Central Park Mall for an appalling program of band music—I meant appealing."

❖ ❖ ❖

SLEEPY-TIME GAL

"This is the Belt Zone broad-resting corporation."

❖ ❖ ❖

CAREER CARETAKER

"That was the latest national and international news direct from the wires of the Associated Press, and now for an item on the brighter side. Hollywood—Jane Russell's husband Bob Waterfield was reported to have said in a recent interview, 'I don't want her to do either housework or cooking. I don't want to endanger her career by bending over a hot stove.' That's the news."

LEADING QUESTION

On a popular program on which occupations are guessed, the contestant was a mattress stuffer. One of the panelists asked this:

"Is your product used by one sex over the other?"

❖ ❖ ❖

BIG FEATURE

"It's a laugh riot, it's a musical treat, it's the film version of the hit broadway show, *Gentlemen Prefer Blondes,* starring Jane Russell and Marilyn Monroe. Yes sir, the big ones come to R. K. O."

❖ ❖ ❖

I SOLEMNLY SWEAR

The microphone is a sensitive instrument and can be dangerous. Listen to this female announcer who forgot the mike was listening.

"And now, audience, here is our special TV Matinee guest that we've all been waiting for—world famous author, lecturer and world traveler, a man about town. Mr. er—er, Mr. . . . Oh! What the hell is his name?"

SPORTSCASTER: "Well, ladies and gentlemen, Cary Middlecoff has done it again, with a one-stroke win over Ben Hogan, and the golf world has a new National Opium champion."

IT'S REFRESHING

"When you're thinking of an all-season thirst quencher, it's a delight—winter or summer—instant White Rose hot or cold Orange Teakoe Pea."

❖ ❖ ❖

FIGURED TO WIN

"As for acting honors it was a walk-away for Ernest Borgnine for his job in *Marty*, and for her work in *The Rose Tattoo* Anna Magnani really deserves to be this year's Anatomy Award winner."

❖ ❖ ❖

BETWEEN THE LINES

Many advertising agencies mark their scripts to show which points to emphasize. Listen to this nervous novice announcer as he does his first commercial:

"Collins Bread is slow baked. Punch this, that means make this sincere. Every inch of each loaf is evenly browned, making for deliciously wholesome super digestible bread. When your grocer asks you, emphasize this. Be sure you say Collins Bread."

THE WONDERFUL WORLD OF NATURE

"Now for a medley of tunes from Walt Disney's films: *High-Diddle-Dee, When You Wish Upon A Star,* and *"I've Seen Everything When I See An Elephant's Fly!"*

⚜ ⚜ ⚜

A REAL TREAT

"At your local R. K. O. theater, starting Monday through Friday, be sure to see Bette Davis in *The Virgin Queen* and *Tonight's the Night*."

⚜ ⚜ ⚜

THEY SAID IT COULDN'T BE DONE

An announcer may sometimes skip a line of his script. This is what happened to a local newsman who did just that:

"And here is another local news item of interest to all you veterans. Tonight there will be a meeting at the Thirty-second Armory sponsored by the Veterans of Foreign Wars. We want to be sure that all those who died for his country will attend."

ANNOUNCER: "Stay tuned in ten seconds when NBC prevents Pinky Lee!"

CALLING ALL GIRLS

"This broadcast is coming to you from the heart of Chicago—The pimp room of the Hotel Ambassador."

❖ ❖ ❖

BOTTOMS UP

"It looks like another big one for Dodie Day. You've just heard the front side of Doris Day's latest hit *Secret Love*. Let's take a look at her backside." (*Embarrassed laughter*) "That is, her *other* side."

❖ ❖ ❖

FAMILY RESEMBLANCE

You have to be careful when you're dealing with Junior on radio. Popular Art Linkletter got tripped up when he asked a youngster, "Who do you resemble most, your mother or father?" "I don't look like, I—I don't look like my mommy or my daddy. I look like the mailman."

SWEET LAND OF LIBERTY

Here's the case of an announcer who confused an earnest plea for savings bonds with a special health bulletin.

"You owe it to yourself to invest in your future. Don't forget to buy government savings bonds. Help stamp out America!"

❖ ❖ ❖

A BIG HIT

"And, friends, if you're in New York you can stop by the Majestic Theater and take in *Fanny*. We understand that Josh Logan's *Fanny* is the biggest thing in town." (*Snickers*.) "I mean it."

❖ ❖ ❖

REST CURE

In a Midwestern town, a bedding concern rented space from a funeral home. Let's listen to one of their commercials.

"So, friends, Beautyrest mattresses are made to give you that extra support to make that night's sleep the best, the most comfortable you've ever had. See for yourself. If you want to insure yourself of the rest you deserve, visit Johnson's Funeral Parlor."

INFLATION

On *Climax*, popular TV dramatic series, a young lady was describing the terrific value of a new automobile.

"Try it for yourself. Your dealer will be glad to give you a chance to get behind the wheel. Feel that power, float on that smooth action—and then be surprised that a car like this can be yours for the amazingly low, unbelievable price of $7,200.00. That should be $2,700.00."

⚜ ⚜ ⚜

NEXT COURSE

Words and phrases often used at home inadvertently find themselves going out over the air waves.

"Let me get this straight. You say when your wife serves dinner she serves dessert first?" "Yeah! My wife does everything ass-backwards."

⚜ ⚜ ⚜

HERE'S LOOKING AT YOU

An announcer doing a commercial for Knickerbocker Beer came on the air after an interview with Jayne Mansfield.

"Next time you're at your local tavern, restaurant or delicatessen, don't forget to" (*Knocks*) "for Bigger Knocker Beer."

WEAR AND TEAR

Bride and Groom is a program that tries to give newlywed couples all sorts of gifts to help their married life get off to a good start.

ANNOUNCER: "And as a final gift for your wedding, we have a wonderful surprise for you. This beautiful original Parisian wedding gown."
BRIDE: "Ooo, I already have my wedding gown. What I really need is a heavy-duty mattress."

❖ ❖ ❖

WOMEN IN WHITE

"Aside from the high degree of surgical efficiency here at the municipal hospital, the student nurses are really something to see. Anybody would welcome a session in bed with one of these beautiful nurses."

❖ ❖ ❖

SOUTHERN COMFORT

Here is a disc jockey who got too mellow for his own good:

"Can't you smell that magnolia in the air? Hm-mmm! And that honeysuckle. Can't you see that Spanish moss weaving from old 'weeping willow'? Uh-huh. I don't have to tell you, it's Stephen Foster music time, with those wonderful songs of the 'Old Souse'."

A commercial TV announcer pulled this classic Blooper:

"This tasty coffee is made from the finest South American tobaccos."

SWISH!

"There have been many ball players who have been able to handle that bat from either the left or right side of the batter's box. But I think most sportswriters will agree that Mickey Mantle is one of the greatest swish hitters of all times. I beg your pardon, I mean Mickey is one of the greatest swith shi..." (*pause*) "...switch hitters of all times, that's Mickey."

❖ ❖ ❖

ATTENTION, RACING FANS

A well-known former jockey, now a sportscaster, came out with this description before a big race, at the Hialeah Race Track.

"One of the unusual sidelights in today's running of the Weidner Handicap here at Hialeah concerns Rock Castle. It wasn't so long ago that this horse broke its leg, and it looked as though they were going to have to shoot the owner."

IT'S A GASSER

Out in the Mid-West local listeners heard this spot announcement for a thriving gasateria:

"Serve yourself the modern way at White's Gasateria. It's just drive up and fill 'er up, and while you're at it take time out for lunch. White's has the best food on the road. White's is the finest spot on the turnpike to eat and get gas!"

❧ ❧ ❧

CALLING BUCK ROGERS

Here's an incident that occurred on a *Man on the Street* program:

INTERVIEWER: "Your fifth trip to New York! Well, you two really do get around."
MAN ON THE STREET: "Yes, we do."
INTERVIEWER: "Well now, what about last year—where did you go then?"
MAN ON THE STREET: "Last year we took a trip around the world, and this year we're going to go somewhere else."

"Hollendale's is open until nine, and don't forget that Hollendale's has the latest maternity fashions for the modern Miss."

SHORT SHORTS

On a local foreign language radio station in New York, this announcement was heard for Schwartz's Department Store:

"With the hot weather upon us now, comfort is the important thing in the July and August dog days. Make it a point to stop in at Schwartz's Department Store for the latest in Bermuda Schwartz."

❖ ❖ ❖

THIS IS POPULARITY?

We take you now to a musical program broadcast by the BBC in London.

"Here's an all time favorite made popular by the famous Miss Jessie Matthews several years back, *Dancing on the Ceiling*. This one surely deserves to be on every British Hit List."

❖ ❖ ❖

BIG BARGAIN

"There are bargain flights every day. You can fly to Miami, Seattle, San Francisco, Montreal. Today for example, you can fly to Dollas, Texas for only thirty-two dallas."

FAMILIAR MELODY

"Here's an old favorite—Tenor with organ, *Looking for a Girl Named Sally.*"

❖ ❖ ❖

ATTENTION, YOU MAPMAKERS

"And here's some news of local interest. From Europe comes word that Private Wilson of Greenpoint, Germany is missing in the Soviet Zone of Brooklyn."

❖ ❖ ❖

INTO THE DEPTHS

"It's seven P.M. Central Standard time. For the latest in movie equipment stop at Harrison's Camera Store, for the latest in Hell and Bowel equipment." (*Off mike*) "Shouldn't that be Bell and Howell?"

❖ ❖ ❖

MOTION PICTURE HIGHLIGHTS

"Exciting, alluring, astounding, exotic! Beginning tomorrow at your neighborhood Loew's theater. Don't fail to see Ava Gardner in *The Bare-Assed Contessa!*"

THE PRICE IS RIGHT

"It's low overhead that does it, so always shop at Robert Hall where prices are high and quality is low."

❖ ❖ ❖

NEXT QUESTION

EMCEE: "All right, all right, and now for our next contestant. What is your name, sir?"
FRIEDMAN: "Jack Friedman."
EMCEE: "Will you step a little closer to the microphone, please. What is your name again?"
FRIEDMAN: "I'm Jack Friedman."
EMCEE: "Thank you, Mr. Friedman, and where are you from?"
FRIEDMAN: "From Brooklyn."
EMCEE: "From Brooklyn—well, welcome to *Sense or Nonsense*. You have chosen for your category the Sense of Sound—that right? Now, you know how to play. We're going to give you certain sounds to identify, and here's the first question. For ten dollars, what is this sound? Now, listen carefully. (*Bong*) All right, now, what is it?"
FRIEDMAN: "That sounds familiar."
EMCEE: "Come on, come on, you've got ten seconds. I'm sure you know."
FRIEDMAN: "Yes, that's Big Ben in Westchester Abbey!"

BUT HE'S A GOOD CATCHER

"And in the world of sports, Yogi Berra the great Yankee catcher was accidently hit in the head by a pitched ball. Yogi was taken to Fordham hospital for X-rays of the head. The X-ray showed nothing."

❖ ❖ ❖

THE WELL-DRESSED BRIDE

On a *Man in the Street* interview program a young lady was asked the reason why she went to New York City. Let's listen to her classic answer.

"I'm getting married next week, and I'm getting my torso ready."

❖ ❖ ❖

AND NOW, ARRIVEDERCI

"And now back to our all-request recorded program. We've had a request for a record by that popular Irish tenor, Mari O'Lanza."

ANNOUNCER: "Folks, try our comfortable beds. I personally stand behind every bed we sell."

WE RUN A CLEAN PLACE

(*Young Dr. Malone*)
"I tell you, Dr. Baxter, there is absolutely no truth in the rumor of flea spitting amongst our physicians at the hospitals."

❖ ❖ ❖

CHECK, PLEASE

(*Soap Opera*)
"You had a cup of coffee, two doughnuts. That makes it 25¢."
"Tell me! How come a dirty girl like you works in a nice clean place like this?"

❖ ❖ ❖

DETOUR FROM PARADISE

PREACHER: "And the Lord says that our deeds each day will lead our way to Heaven."

ANNOUNCER: "Ladies and gentlemen, we regret that our time has run out and we are unable to continue our services from St. Joseph's Cathedral. We now bring you a program of recorded music. Our first selection, *Heaven Can Wait*."

COUNT-DOWN

EMCEE: "What did you say your name was, ma'am?"
SARA JANE COLLINS: "Sara Jane Collins."
EMCEE: "And what brings you down to Florida, down to these parts?"
SARA JANE COLLINS: "Well, we're stationed at Cape Canaveral, you know . . . where they have those secret projects?"
EMCEE: "Is there anything you can tell us about it, or is that all classified?"
SARA JANE COLLINS: "Well, that's all classified, sir."
EMCEE: "Well, can you 'least tell us what your husband does?"
SARA JANE COLLINS: "Well, my husband's a guided muscle expert!"

❖ ❖ ❖

FLASH!

"And here's the latest news from Hollywood, the movie capital. Just saw Jayne Mansfield's new picture *Will Success Spoil Rock Hunter?*, and I have surprising news for those of you who never thought Jayne had any acting ability. She gives a splendid performance. I wonder how Jayne's knockers feel now?"

(*OPA spot announcement*)
"Ladies, take your fat cans down to the corner butcher."

SPORTS LOVER

ANNOUNCER: "Pardon me, sir, may I ask your name and where you are from?"

SOL: "Yeah, I'm Sol Bernstein, I'm from Philadelphia. I just came in for the game today."

ANNOUNCER: "Well, it was a wonderful game, wasn't it?"

SOL: "Yeah, that Mickey Mantle is sure some ballplayer."

ANNOUNCER: "Tell me Sol—if I may call you Sol—are you rooting for the Yankees or the Indians?"

SOL: "Well, neither of them. I'm an Athletic supporter."

❖ ❖ ❖

TEMPOS FUGIT

The Dorsey brothers, Tommy and Jimmy, had trumpeter Louis Armstrong as featured guest on their television show *Stage Show*. The Dorseys were about to play a number with Louis when Satchmo set the tempo in this fashion.

"Okay, you cats, now just play the simple mustard jazz not too slow and not too fast . . . just half fast."

QUICK TURNOVER

Here's the way a young disc jockey introduced Eddie Fisher's latest recording:

"And now, girls, in response to your numerous requests, we give you Eddie Fisher's *Fanny* on a brand new platter."

♣ ♣ ♣

WELCOME, FRIEND

"And here's some news of local interest. Our neighbors over in Columbia, Tennessee—the largest out-door mule market in the world—had a Jackass Parade, headed by the Governor."

♣ ♣ ♣

MIDNIGHT SNACK

"And stay tuned for the late movie, Alexander Dumas' immortal classic *The Count of Monte Crisco*, starring Robert Donut."

IT'S THE GOSSIPEL

"Stay tuned to this station for your evening's entertainment. Immediately following Walter Winchell, hear the current dope in Hollywood—Listen to Louella Parsons."

⚜ ⚜ ⚜

CLEAN UP

"So, if you have washday troubles, put an end to them with a really modern detergent. . . . Send immediately for a free dirty day's supply."

⚜ ⚜ ⚜

DENTAL PROBLEM

(*After jingle, announcer cut in*)
"Yes! You'll wonder where your teeth went when you brush your yellow with Pepsodent."

⚜ ⚜ ⚜

JAIL BAIT

"Now, stay tuned to America's favorite penal program, *What's My Line.*"

HEAR! HEAR!

"You've just heard, *There's No Business Like Show Business* sung by the robust voice of Ethel Murmer."

❖ ❖ ❖

WHAT'S IN IT FOR ME?

(Announcer, in solemn voice)
"So, remember friends, Parker's Funeral Home at 4th and Maple for the finest in funeral arrangements . . . and now the lucky winner of our deep freeze."

❖ ❖ ❖

RAPID DEVELOPMENT

"And here's an item of local interest. A baby boy was born to Mr. and Mrs. Daniel Horton of Edgemont Drive of this city while they were on a quick trip to Europe. Mr. Horton mixed business with pleasure."

An announcer on a local radio station, in doing a commercial for one of the local banks, asked the audience to "stop in and join the Blonde-a-Month Club."

A NEW LEAF

(*Commercial on two pages*)
"Tums will give you instant relief and assure you no indigestion or distress during the night . . . So try Tums and go to sleep with a broad . . ." (*turn page*) ". . . smile."

❖ ❖ ❖

BON APPETIT

"And now ladies, with Reduce-Aids, that new sensational weight control pill, you can successfully lose weight, and still eat three hearty males a day."

❖ ❖ ❖

NICE ORDEAL

"I want you to know that the horses and cattle I bought from you were Grade A stock. It's been a business doing pleasure with you."

❖ ❖ ❖

IT'S A PLEASURE

"This unprecedented drop in school attendance was due to the pleasant outbreak of Asiatic Flu."

BATTLE OF THE SEXES

"And, in the world of golf, some of the favorites in the National Open are ... Slammin' Sammy Snead and the Dentist from Memphis Mary Giddlecoff."

❖ ❖ ❖

A SMASHER

"A highlight of the county fair at Middletown was the First Prize $50.00 Savings Bond awarded to Mrs. Louise Proctor by the Stevens Baking Co. as the winner of their annual Bed Breaking Contest."

❖ ❖ ❖

HOLLYWOOD HIGH LIFE

Hollywood stars are usually faced with the problem of losing weight before starting a new picture. But not in the case of talented Shelley Winters, who in her latest picture, *The Diary of Anne Frank,* found that she had to gain 53 pounds. When asked how this was done, she replied she had to go on a very strict high colonic diet.

An announcer on a newscast told of this incident:

"Word has just reached us that a home-made blonde exploded in the Roxy Theatre this morning."

"This conclees . . .

　　this concloos . . .

　　　　　that is all!"

ABOUT MR. BLOOPER

High on a hill overlooking the Ramapo Mountains in Central Valley, New York sits a modern redwood house which is the home of radio-TV producer, Kermit Schafer. This attractive and interesting home, which has been featured in such national magazines as *McCall's*, has become a veritable listening post for radio and TV Bloopers.

On a visit inside, you will see a battery of built-in tape recorders which are constantly in operation in the process of monitoring several programs simultaneously. With all of this equipment Kermit Schafer, or "Mr. Blooper," as he is sometimes referred to, capitalizes on the mistakes of others.

Until recent years radio and TV performers who made a verbal fluff on the air were only concerned with the people who might be listening at the moment. Almost everyone can remember hearing some such error and enjoying it heartily at the time. Radio and TV performers are so nearly letter-perfect that their boners strike us as very amusing; but now, when someone commits a Blooper on the air, he is less concerned with all the people who heard it than with the man who might have been listening—that man being Kermit Schafer.

Kermit Schafer began his career as a radio and TV producer, having produced several top radio and TV network programs. Over the years Mr. Schafer has had experience in all phases of the industry. As a hobby, he began to collect "fluffs" which had been made by radio and TV performers. He continued his collection during his four years in the Air Force—and after his return to civilian life. With the rise of the tape recorder to technical perfection, Schafer was launched on a new career.

It occurred to him that the public in general would have as much fun and entertainment from this unique type of material as his private circle of friends had. His collection started with the classic Harry Von Zell fluff introduction in the early days of radio, when he blurted out, "Ladies and gentlemen, the President of the United States, Hoobert Heever." The collection continued to include modern-day television.

Schafer was the first to dub these twists of the tongue "Blooper"—a word which has already been added to the American language, and he is rapidly becoming more and more associated with this term as was the Reverend Spooner who was responsible for the word "Spoonerism."

Several colleges throughout the country are using the Blooper recordings in their speech classes, finding that they serve an educational purpose and, at the same time, brighten the course for the students.

As he set about building his collection Schafer culled the record archives of stations coast to coast and taped some of the most hilarious Bloopers ever heard in the past 25 years.

Within a short time Schafer had gleaned enough material to fill a book called, appropriately enough, *Your Slip Is Showing*, published by Grayson and included in this enlarged Crest edition. Encouraged by its success, Schafer turned his tape recorders on the outpouring of radio and TV sounds and came up with a record album called *Pardon My Blooper* and released by Jubilee Records.

The public reaction to this first album was phenomenal. Somehow or other, Schafer had managed to tickle the national funnybone by ribbing some of the most sacrosanct voices heard on radio and television. People enjoyed hearing their favorite announcers and stars take a little slip on the verbal banana peel.

Some of the nation's top magazines such as *Coronet* and *Reader's Digest* carried excerpts from his collection. Schafer is now writing a regular monthly exclusive feature on Bloopers in *McCall's* magazine, and a daily syndicated newspaper column through Editor's Syndicate over his by-line, entitled *Bloopers*, appearing in newspapers coast to coast. He is also being booked on a coast-to-coast lecture tour which is called *Blooperama*. Schafer takes his tape recorder along with him and entertains all types of audiences with his fabulous Blooper collection.

As Schafer produced more record albums, *Pardon My Blooper* Vol. 1 through 8, he became nationally known as the definitive authority on Bloopers, and he is now the central clearing house for this type of material. People from all over the world send him verbal boners as well as recorded ones. In addition to these contributions, Schafer has used his many contacts in the radio and television fields to secure permission to use original recordings which ordinarily would not be made available to anyone. Celebrities call him as soon as they have committed any Bloopers which will add to his collection.

Schafer's audience has no bounds as to appeal; down-to-earth everyday radio and TV fans comprise the largest part of his following. They seem to find this authentic type of humor, based on truth, far funnier than any type of contrived joke. His fans from all walks of life are quick to write glowing testimonials lauding the good taste, manner and treatment in which the subject is handled.

Amongst Schafer's staunchest fans are some of the victims of the classic boners. As a producer-director, he has often felt the anguish and pain when a blooper was committed on any of his programs. He therefore dedicates his works as a sympathetic tribute to the victims with the hope that they find consolation and proof that they are not alone. They realize that his works are meant to be funny, not critical.

> *Send Bloopers to:*
> KERMIT SCHAFER
> THE BLOOPER SNOOPER CLUB
> 905 FAIRWAY DRIVE
> MIAMI BEACH, FLORIDA 33141